WAY TO PLAY:
BLUEGRASS GUITAR SOLO

Jay Hicks, Philip Groeber

Contents

Note: The pieces in this book are composed by the authors unless otherwise indicated.

Production: Frank J. Hackinson

Production Coordinator: Philip Groeber

Cover Design and Interior Art: Andi Whitmer

Engraving: Tempo Music Press, Inc.

Printer: Tempo Music Press, Inc.

Recording Credits: Jay Hicks (guitar)
Seabie Ewer (banjo/mandolin)
Skylar Gandy (fiddle)
Rob Sylvester (bass)

Engineer: Seabie Ewer

ISBN-13: 978-1-61928-135-6

What is Bluegrass Music?

Bluegrass music is an American musical style that draws its roots from European and African musical traditions. Bluegrass evolved in the early twentieth century, with much of its characteristic sound coming from Appalachia. Appalachian folk songs and fiddle tunes were heavily influenced by the music of the Northern European ancestors who came to America. However, some of the music from this tradition is distinguished as mountain music, and uses instrumentation, such as the dulcimer, not common to bluegrass.

Bluegrass is typically considered a sub-category within country music. Typical instrumentation in Bluegrass music includes the banjo (an instrument with an African heritage), the mandolin, the fiddle, the upright bass, and the guitar. The steel resonator guitar (particularly the Dobro) is also frequently used. There is no drummer in a bluegrass band, the only rhythm needed is provided by the other instrumentalists.

The name "Bluegrass" was not applied to the style until the mid-twentieth century. Bill Monroe, known as the father of bluegrass music, named his band "The Blue Grass Boys," drawing on the nickname of his home state of Kentucky (the bluegrass state). The band was so popular that people began calling the music "bluegrass." Bluegrass music is characterized by personal and storied lyrical content, with three-part and sometimes four-part vocal harmonies. The vocal sound of bluegrass is described as a "high and lonesome" sound. Instrumentally, bluegrass is characterized by strong rhythms and virtuosic soloing.

Fiddle tunes are often adapted for bluegrass instruments. In a typical tune, several instruments will take a solo (or break), improvising over the form of the tune. Traditional folk songs, fiddle tunes, spirituals, and hymns are commonly adapted for bluegrass instrumentation and vocals, and many have become a part of the standard bluegrass repertoire. The guitar was primarily a rhythm instrument in early bluegrass bands, and did little soloing. However, in the second half of the twentieth century many great flatpicking guitarists, such as Doc Watson and Tony Rice, established the guitar as a legitimate solo instrument in bluegrass music.

G1053

Equipment

Guitars

Bluegrass can be played on any type of guitar. If a guitar has six strings and working frets, then techniques and playing styles unique to bluegrass can be played on it. Most professional bluegrass guitarists play steel string acoustic guitars. They often use the **dreadnought** body style, because of the increased volume that it can generate.

Amplification

While some contemporary players use acoustic guitars with built-in electronics for amplification, most still use a microphone when performing to boost the volume level. Because of the natural "loudness" of other bluegrass instruments (particularly the banjo), generating plenty of volume on the guitar, without losing the natural acoustic sound is an important factor.

Strings

Bronze strings (either Phosphor Bronze or 80/20 Bronze) are the strings of choice for most bluegrass guitarists playing steel-string guitars. For a beginning guitarist a light gauge set of strings is a good choice. Some seasoned players choose to use medium gauge strings to increase the volume level of the guitar. It is important to know the recommended strings for a guitar. Some guitars are not designed to support the added tension created by medium or heavy gauge strings.

Picks

Bluegrass guitar is considered a "flatpicking" style. Most bluegrass guitarists use a flat-pick, because of the need to alternate stroke direction quickly. The heavier the gauge (thickness) of a pick, the more control the player has. For players who are not accustomed to using thicker picks, a medium gauge between .8 and 1 would be a good starting point.

Capo

A **capo** is used to effectively move the end of the neck up, raising the pitch of the open strings. Bluegrass guitarists frequently use a capo to accommodate the desired "keys" (or tonal centers) of singers or other instrumentalists.

Our Top Ten Bluegrass Recordings

We recommend you start listening to these excellent artists and also keep your ears open to as many bluegrass recordings as you can. You will come up with your own top ten list!

The Bluegrass Album Band
(The Bluegrass Album Compact Disc)

Bill Monroe
(20th Century Masters: The Millenium Collection)

J.D.Crowe
(J.D. Crowe)

O Brother Where Art Thou?
(Soundtrack - Various Artists)

Flatt and Scruggs
(The Complete Mercury Sessions)

Tony Rice
(Manzinita)

Alison Krauss and Union Station
(Live)

Ricky Skaggs and Kentucky Thunder
(Bluegrass Rules!)

Jimmy Martin
(King of Bluegrass)

Will the Circle Be Unbroken
(The Nitty Gritty Dirt Band and Friends)

Bluegrass Essentials

A year of guitar study is recommended before beginning this book. Successfully completing **Everybody's Guitar Method 1** or an equivalent is a good idea. Reading skills of notation and guitar tablature along with knowledge of basic chords and strumming techniques are required, and experience in ensemble playing is a plus.

FIRST POSITION NOTES

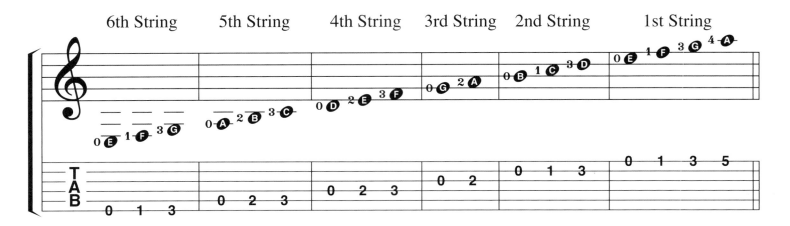

Terms in bold throughout the book are important concepts for you to know and understand. Research these terms to further expand your knowledge of music.

The **Everybody's Guitar Series** consists of several excellent supplemental publications that can improve your note-reading skills. Visit www.fjhmusic.com/guitar.htm for more information.

CHORDS

Knowledge of First Position chords, chord types (major, minor, minor sevenths, etc.), and the ability to play elementary barre chords are necessary. A good chord book such as **Everybody's Basic Guitar Chords** is recommended for further movable barre chord study.

TRACK NO.

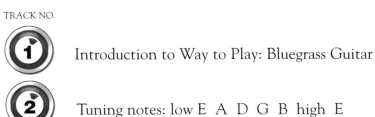

1   Introduction to Way to Play: Bluegrass Guitar

2   Tuning notes: low E A D G B high E

G1053

The Key of G

The Key of G can easily be identified by the F♯ in the **key signature**, which indicates that all of the F notes will be played sharp. Memorize the notes of the G major scale below. The melodies to most of the songs you know are built on major scales.

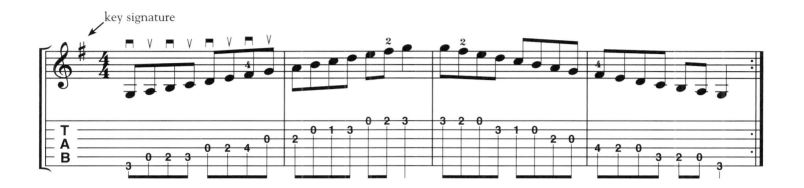

CHORDS AND STRUMMING

PRIMARY CHORDS IN THE KEY OF G

The term primary chords refers to the most commonly used chords in any key. These chords are identified by numbers as well as letters. The numbers refer to the letter name of the chord as it appears in a major scale. In the Key of G these chords are G (I), C (IV), and D (V). Many bluegrass musicians refer to chords by number only.

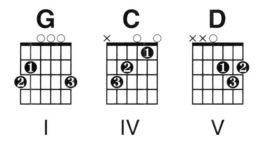

The most basic strum used in bluegrass music is the root-strum pattern. When using this pattern the lowest-sounding root note of the chord is played first, followed by a down-stroke strum of the chord.

Use the primary chords in the key of G to practice the root-strum technique.

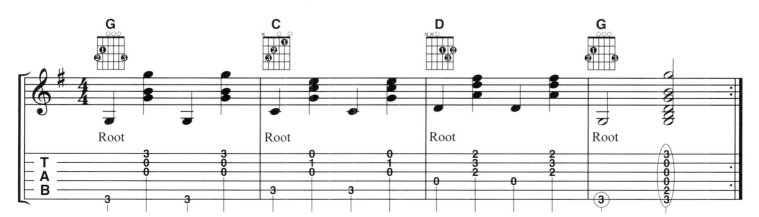

The Key of C

The **Key of C** can easily be identified by the the key signature because there are no sharps or flats in the C major scale. Memorize the notes of the C major scale below. Be sure to identify what key a new song is in before you start playing!

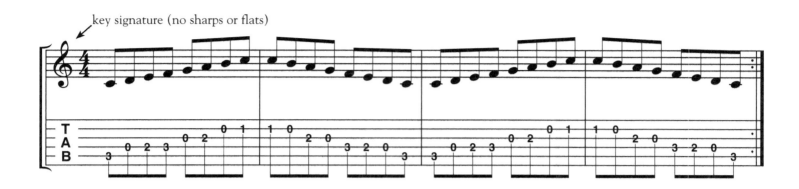

CHORDS AND STRUMMING

PRIMARY CHORDS IN THE KEY OF C

In the Key of C these chords are C (I), F (IV), and G (V).

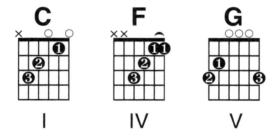

Use the primary chords in the key of C to practice the root-strum pattern.

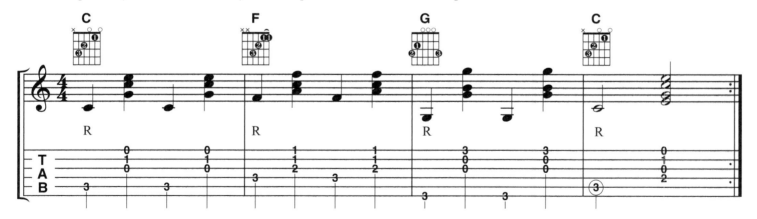

Tech Tip Practice until you are comfortable playing the scales, primary chords, and strums in the Keys of G and C. These basic music elements are used throughout this book.

Traditional

Use *The Crawdad Song* to practice the root-strum technique. Use downstrokes on the root and the strum. To make the **rhythm** accompaniment (rhythm guitar) easy to read, this book will omit the 5-line staff and will use only the TAB staff for the songs.

Be sure to practice the **melody** (or tune) of the songs, in addition to the accompaniment. Knowing the melody is a valuable tool in anticipating (feeling) the chord changes.

In bluegrass music lingo, the root-strum pattern is often called a "Boom-chuck" pattern, because the root creates a "Boom" effect while the strum creates a "chuck" effect.

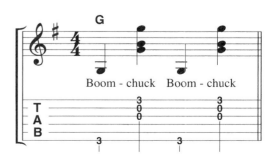

Changing The Boom, Part 1

Now try a different variation of the root-strum technique. Alternate the root with the 5th of each chord. The 5th refers to the fifth note of the major scale with the same letter name as the chord. On the C chord, alternate the 3rd finger between the 5th and 6th strings on the 3rd fret, notes C (R) and G (5th).

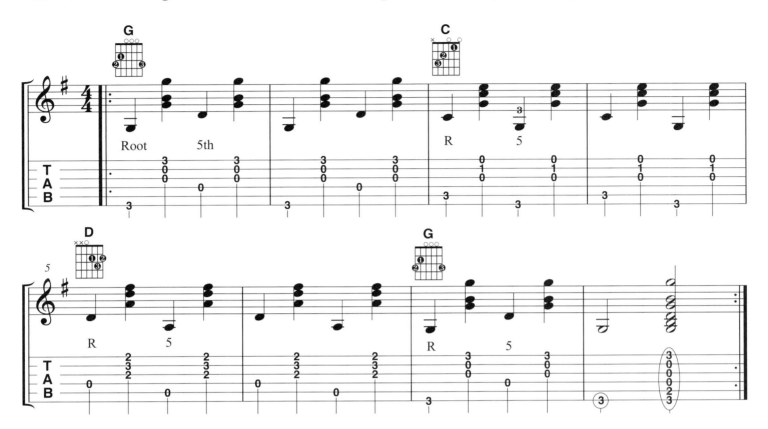

Tech Tip — When strumming using the root and the fifth on the C chord, be sure to leave your first and second fingers down. Your third finger will move back and forth from the fifth to the sixth strings.

Bluegrass Breakdown — Alternate fingerings can be used to make the chord changes a little easier. For example, the new fingering for the G chord can help you change back and forth from the C chord. There is not a right or wrong way to finger a chord. Use whatever works best for you.

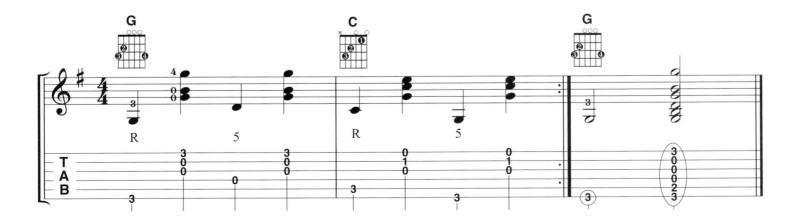

G1053

No Hiding Place Down Here

Traditional

Kick It Off

one anna
two anna ...

No Hiding Place Down Here is a traditional Gospel song written in the early 1900s. The Original Carter Family recorded the definitive version in 1934.

Changing The Boom, Part 2

In addition to the root and 5th of the chord, the 3rd can also be used to add variety to the root-strum technique. Alternate the root with the 3rd or the 5th of the chord. Notice that using 3rds and 5ths can give a sense of leading into the root of the next chord.

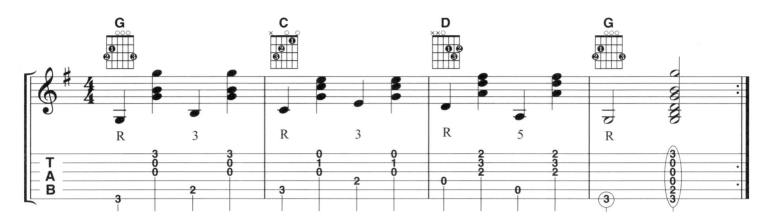

Front Porch Swing ⑤

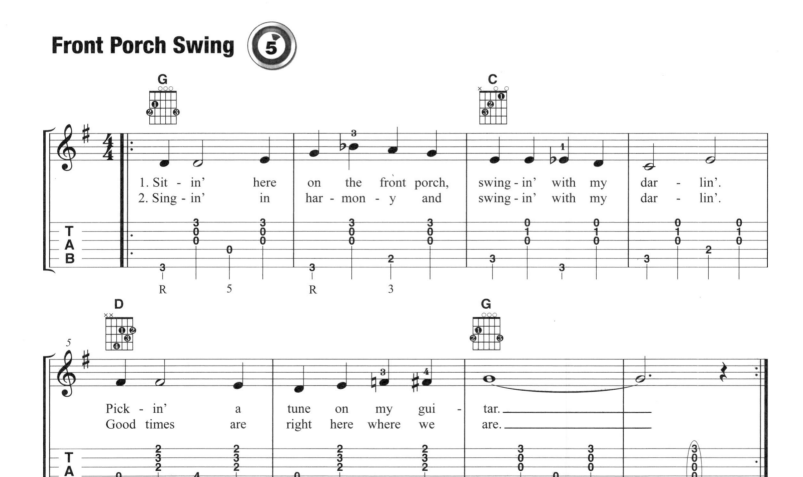

1. Sit - in' here on the front porch, swing - in' with my dar - lin'.
2. Sing - in' in har - mon - y and swing - in' with my dar - lin'.

Pick - in' a tune on my gui - tar._____
Good times are right here where we are._____

In measure 5 of *Front Porch Swing*, the 3rd of the D chord is played at the 4th fret on the 4th string, using the 4th finger (as indicated in the diagram).

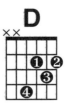

G1053

Traditional

Kick It Off

Banks of the Ohio was recorded by The Carter Family, Doc Watson, Dolly Parton, Johnny Cash, and many others.

THE HAMMER-ON

When two or more *ascending* notes are connected by a slur, a technique called the **hammer-on** is used. Play the first note with the pick, then drop the left-hand finger (like a hammer) onto the string to sound the second note.

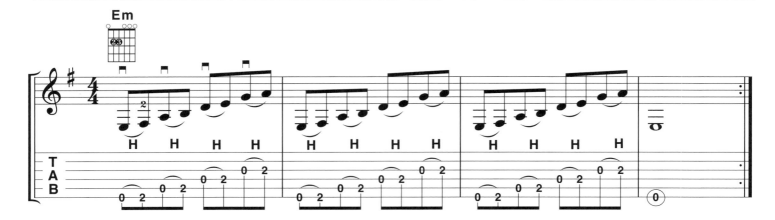

THE PULL-OFF

When two or more *descending* notes are connected by a slur, a technique called the **pull-off** is used. Play the first note with the pick, then pull the left-hand finger off (towards the floor) to sound the second note.

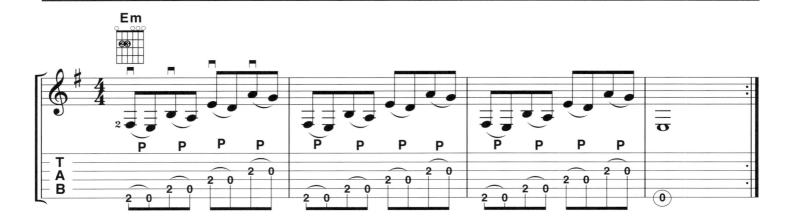

Hammerin' and a-Pullin' ⑦

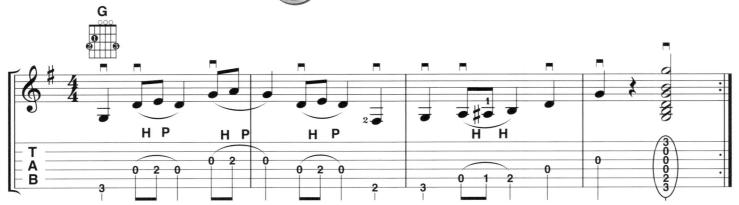

Tech Tip

Hammerin' and a-Pullin' combines a hammer-on (H) and a pull-off (P) in one motion. Be sure to only pick the string one time for each slur. Listen to the audio track often and match the sound that you hear. Hammer-ons and pull-offs are very important guitar techniques in bluegrass music.

The G run is the most common **lick** used in bluegrass music. It can be used as a fill-in, an intro, or an ending. There are many variations of runs. You will see the G Run used with other chord names as well, such as "G Run" in C. The important part of the G run is not that the run is in G but that it is a certain sequence of notes that can be started on different pitches.

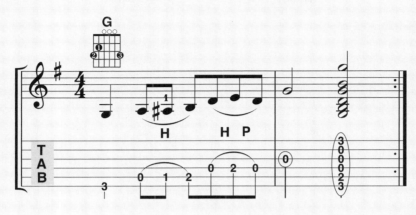

Basic G Run

Expanded G Run

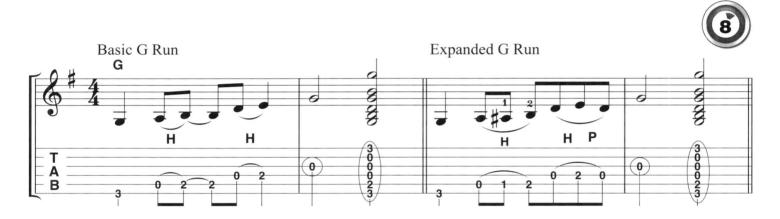

Basic "G Run" in C

Expanded "G Run" in C

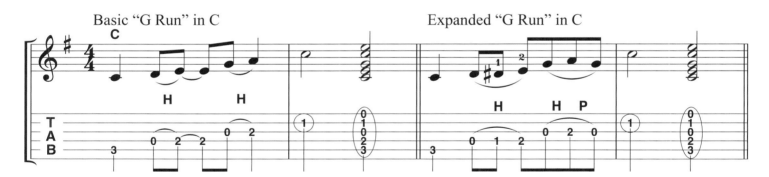

Basic "G Run" in D

Expanded "G Run" in D

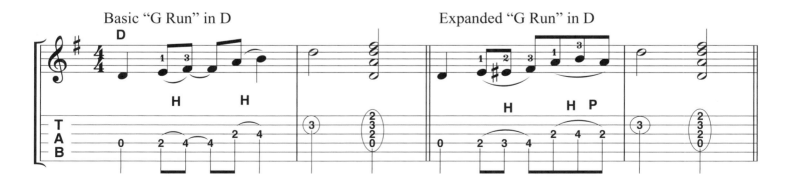

Changing The Boom, Part 3

When playing rhythm guitar, notes can be used to introduce a chord change. A common practice is to borrow one of the functions of the bass player and connect the notes between the roots. Below are examples of connecting the roots, the G run, and an ending.

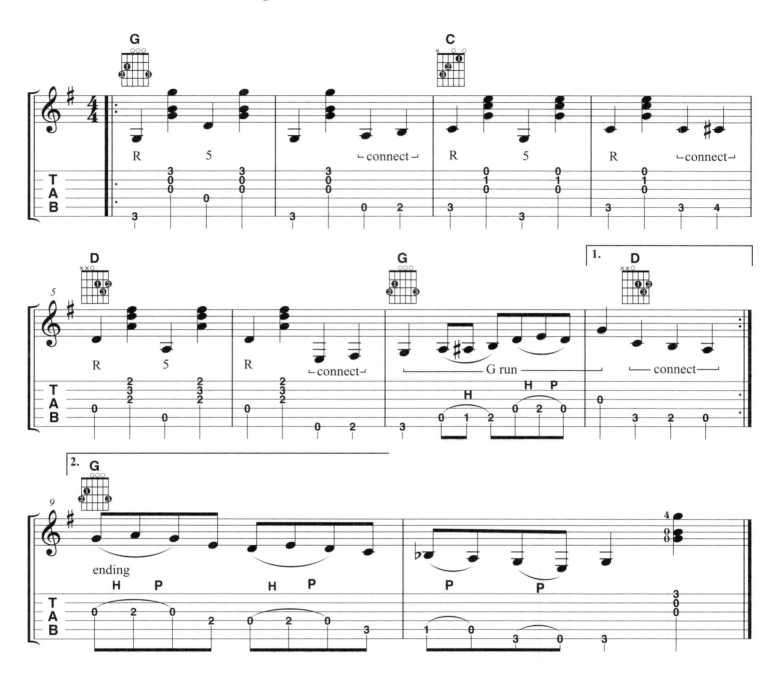

Play all of the *Changing the Boom* examples often, and memorize them as soon as you can. Bluegrass musicians have a lot of fun coming up with creative ways to connect chords, add runs, and come up with new intros and endings. As you move along in this book, you will come up with your own ideas.

G1053

Roll in My Sweet Baby's Arms

Traditional

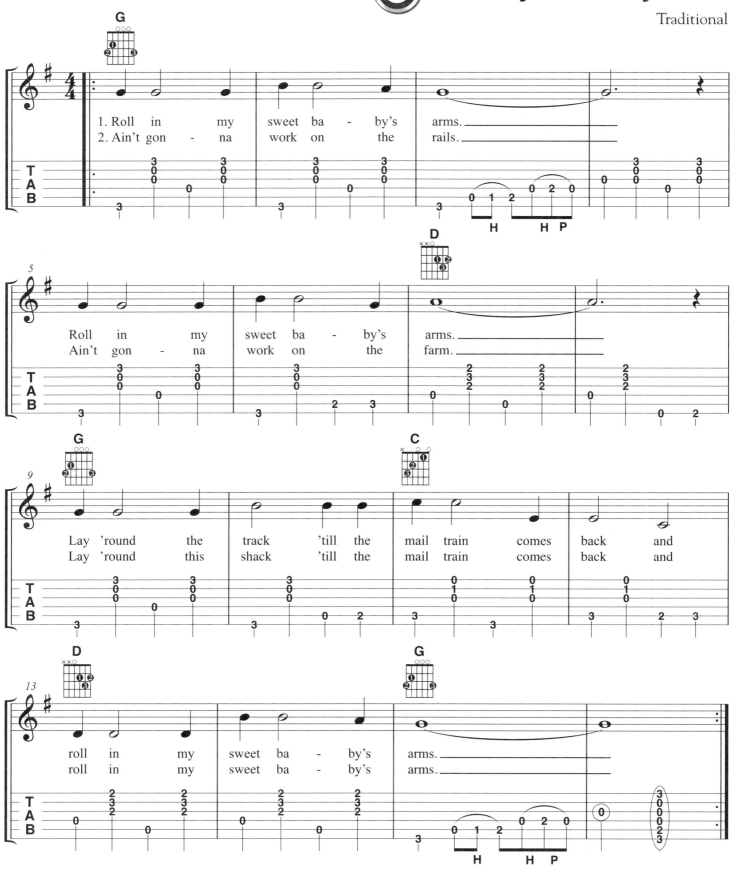

Listen to as many bluegrass recordings as you can. Go to live bluegrass music concerts, festivals, and jam sessions in your area.

All the Good Times 🔟

Traditional

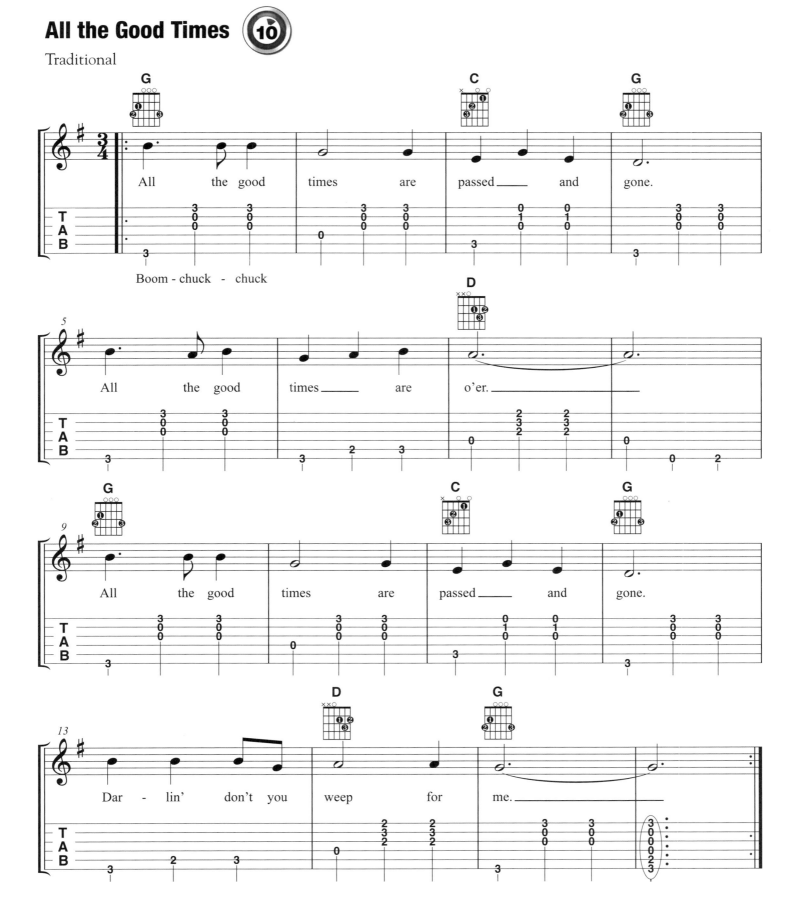

All the Good Times is in 3/4 time, which is often called a waltz. Be sure you feel 3 beats a measure when playing both the melody and the accompaniment.

The accompaniment pattern in 3/4 time is referred to as "Boom-chuck-chuck."

Shave And A Haircut Ending

Another effective ending is "Shave and a Haircut". Using it usually brings a smile to everyone's face!

The Basics

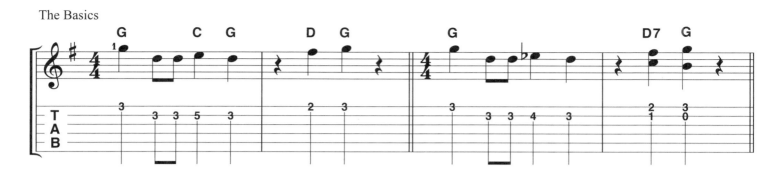

Variations

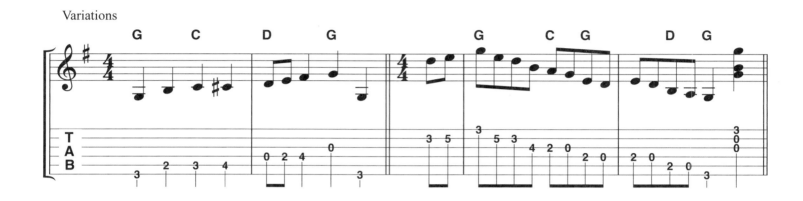

Variations in
the Key of C

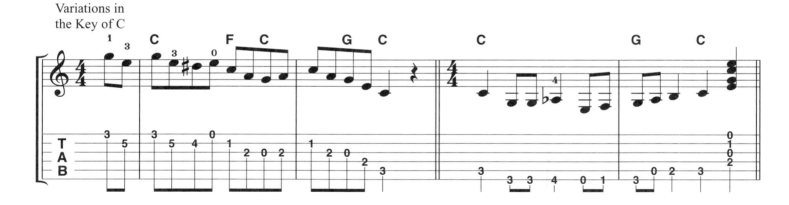

Shifting Gears 12

Start off at a slow, steady tempo. Each day increase your speed a little, keeping a steady pulse. Alternate using downstrokes (⊓) and upstrokes (V) throughout. The use of a metronome will help with your technique. Start at 100 bpm (beats per minute) and gradually increase the tempo.

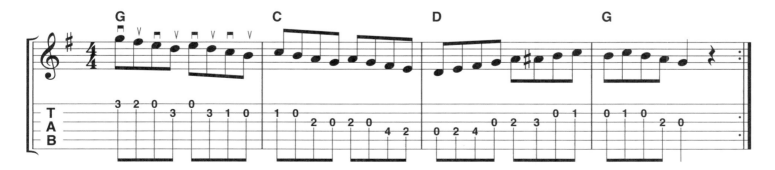

Lonesome Road Blues

Traditional

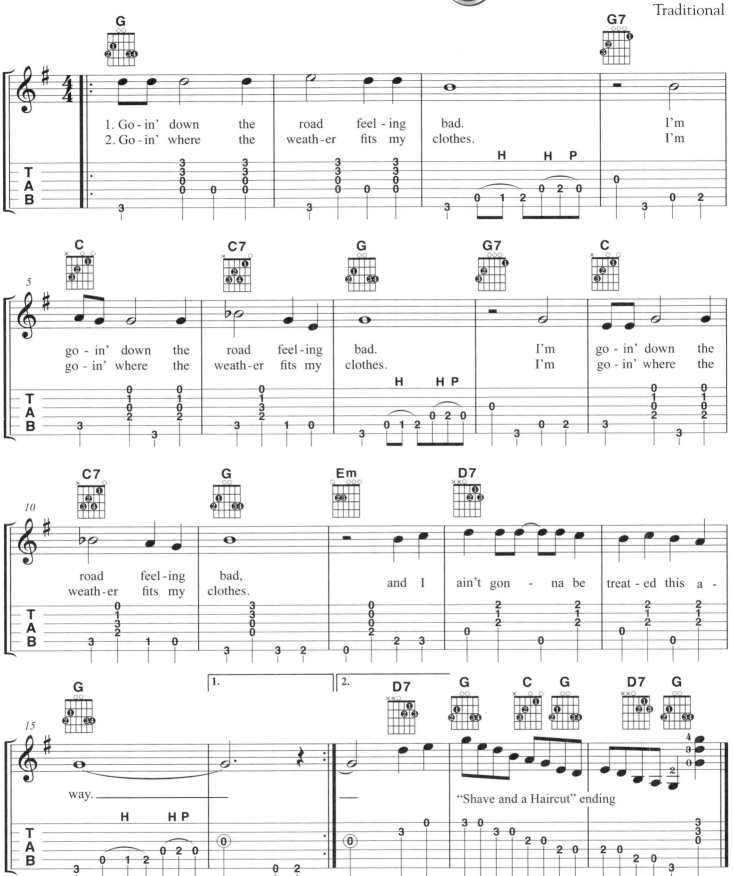

Lonesome Road Blues uses a variation of the G chord.

Introduction To Soloing

In bluegrass music, like jazz, instruments in the band often take turns soloing (or "taking a break"). Solos can be memorized, but are often improvised. Let's look at ways to develop soloing skills.

Licks are not just for ending phrases and songs when you're playing rhythm. Licks are an important part of improvised solos. The G run in G, C, and D, along with variations of the "Shave and a Haircut" lick are tools you already have in your soloing toolbag.

Bluegrass Breakout

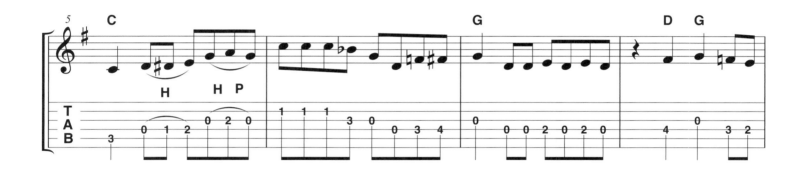

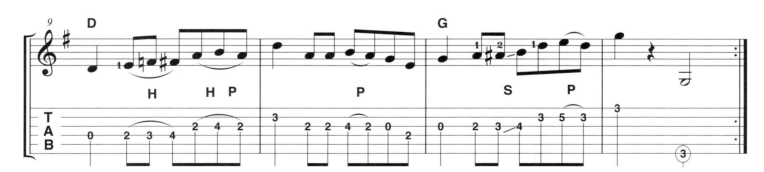

N.C. indicates No Chord. The rhythm stops while the soloist continues to play.

Name the licks that are used in *Bluegrass Breakout*.

measure 5 _____

measures 7-8 _____

measures 9-10 _____

measures 11-12 _____

Choose from:
G run
"G run" in C
"G run" in D
Shave and a Haircut

G1053

SCALES

Each type of **scale** can be useful in creating a bluegrass solo. Play each of the following scales several times slowly, listening to the subtle differences between each.

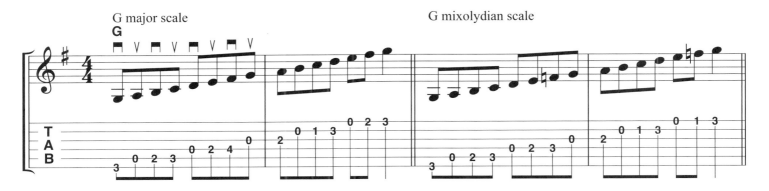

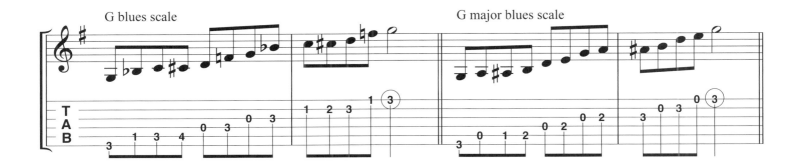

Composers and improvisers use notes from scales to create interesting melodies. Committing the scales to memory helps when improvising solos. However, there's more to creating a memorable solo than just playing scales. Scales provide a basis for note sequences that work in the key of a tune.

The bluegrass soloist should use notes from appropriate scales to create melodic ideas by using interesting rhythmic patterns, note repetitions, and even rests.

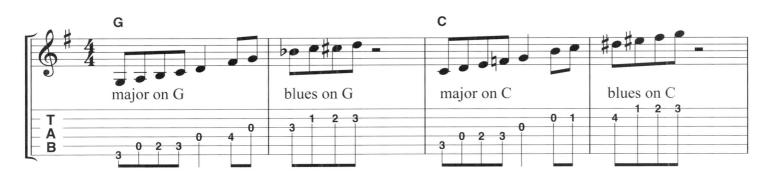

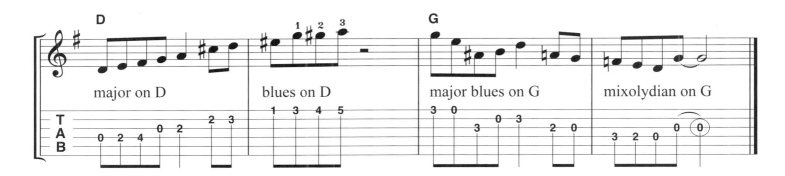

Variations on Cripple Creek uses all four of the G scales that you've learned.

Variations on Cripple Creek

Traditional

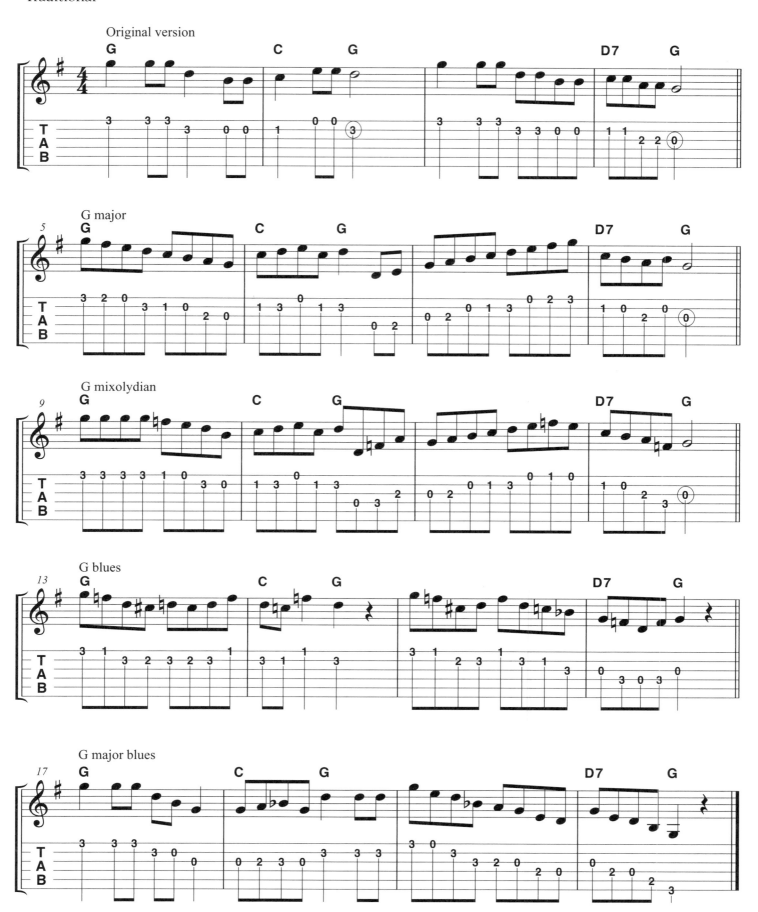

Playing Melody

When you're playing a song which has lyrics, knowing the melody that goes with the lyrics is a good place to start developing a solo. Here's a melodic passage from the song *Somebody Touched Me* in the key of G major. Play this several times to get the melody "in your head." Be sure to listen to the audio track of this passage.

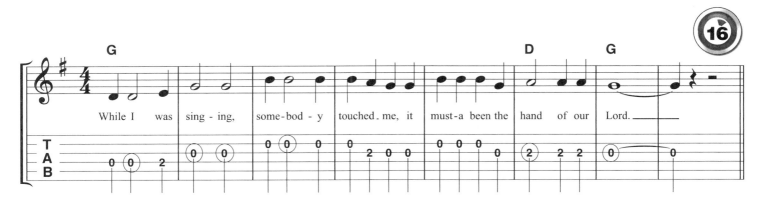

Taking the melody and varying or expanding the rhythms can help us to begin to improvise a solo over the melody.

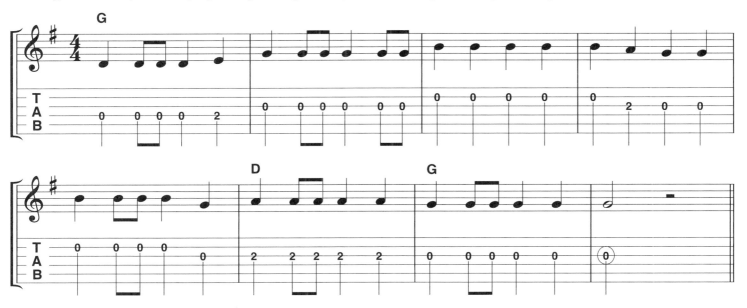

Now we'll add and substitute some notes of the G major scale, as well as adding a G run at the end to create more variation in the improvised solo.

G1053

Play the melody of *Somebody Touched Me*, followed by a break created in the style of an improvised solo.

Somebody Touched Me

Traditional

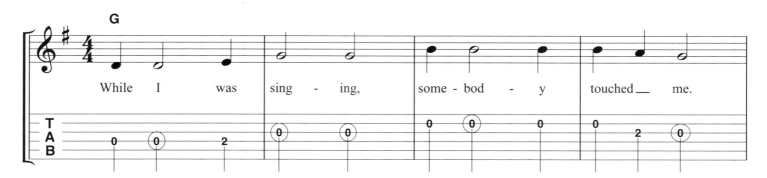

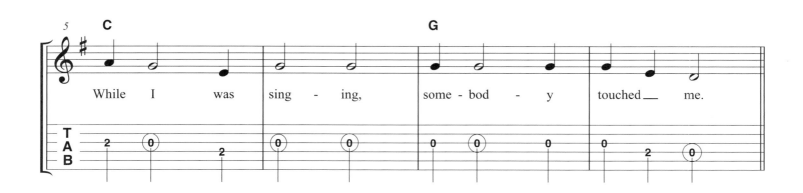

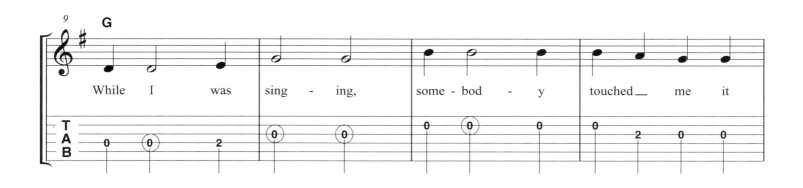

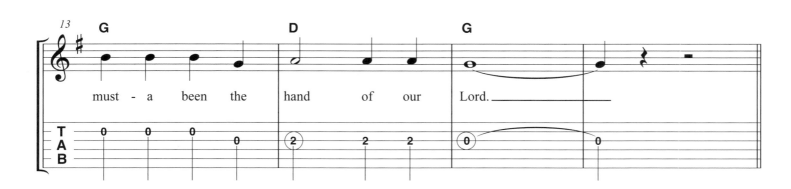

Break

Melodic rhythm variation

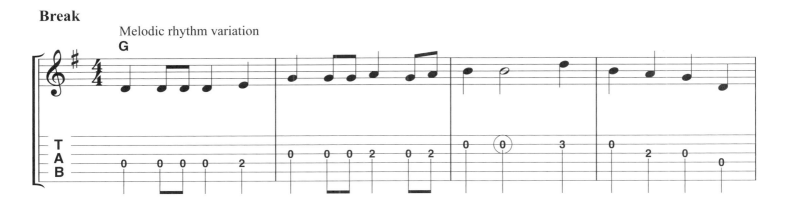

"G Run" in C   G major blues

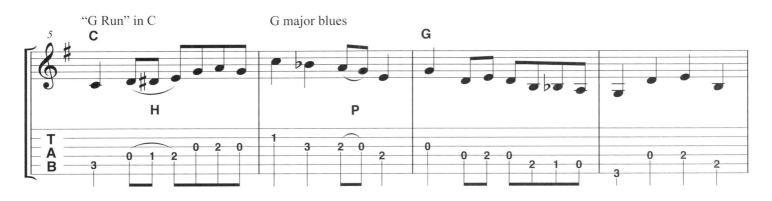

G major blues

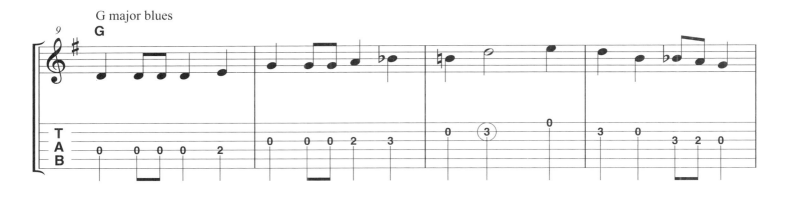

G blues   G mixolydian   G Run

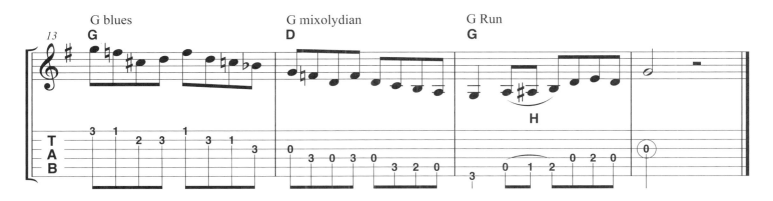

Feelin' Good

1. Any type of **rest** designates a period of silence. Be sure to **dampen** (keep from vibrating) your strings for rests.

2. **Let ring** indicates to allow the strings to vibrate as long as possible. Many runs using open strings sound like a banjo when played this way. Some of the "New Grass" players refer to this sound as *floaties*.

G1053

19 Under the Double Eagle

Josef Franz Wagner

Guitar Solo

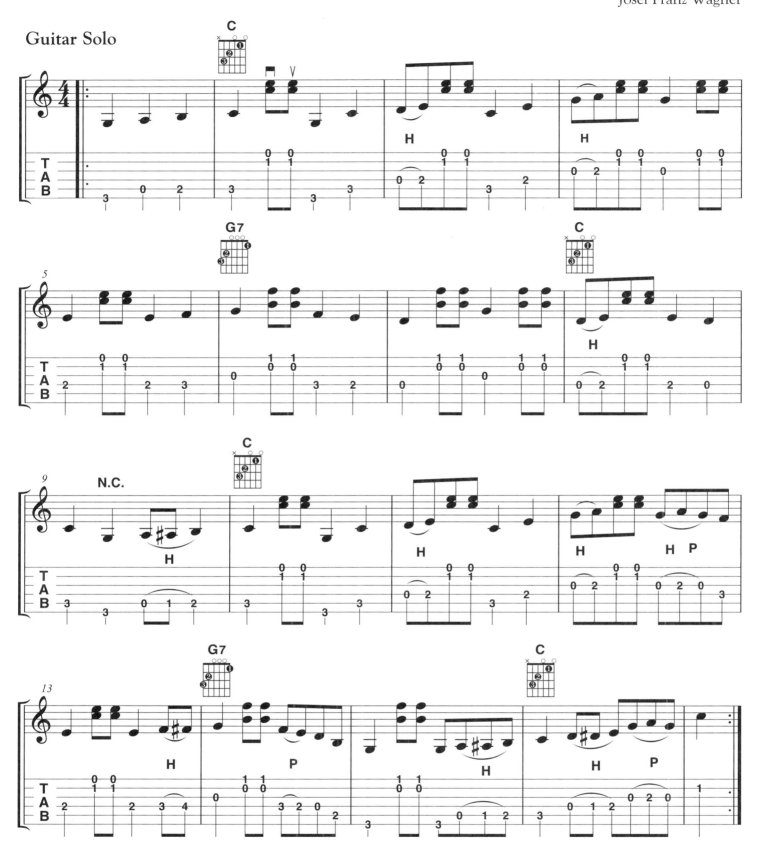

Kick It Off

one anna two anna …

Under the Double Eagle is a bluegrass song that you *must* be familiar with. Research the story about the experience of Happy Traum (an American folk musician) as he was hitchhiking.

Whiskey Before Breakfast

Traditional Fiddle Tune

Guitar Solo

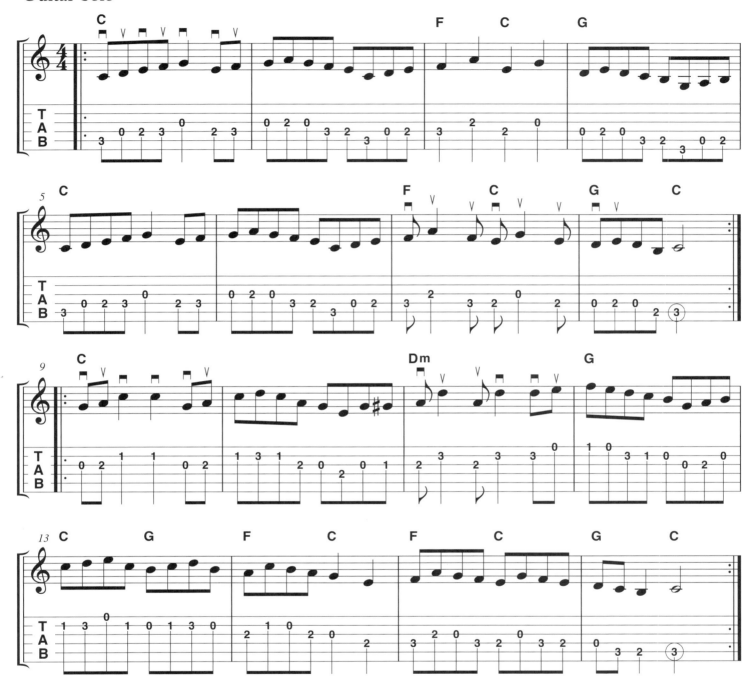

Licks (like the *Shave and a Haircut* and *G run* licks) are often added to the end of a tune, after the melody has been played the last time. Try adding the "JH lick" below after *Whiskey Before Breakfast*, or any song in the key of C. Experiment with both fingering options.

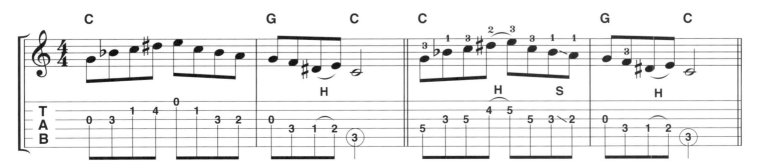

Double Stops

"**Double stops**" (from fiddle lingo) occur when two notes are played at the same time, creating **harmony**. When flatpicking, two adjacent strings are played with a down stroke to create the double stop. The next adjacent string in the downward motion can be used to stop the pick. This is referred to as a rest stroke. Play the following double stop exercise on the third and second strings. Let the pick stop (rest) on top of the first string each time.

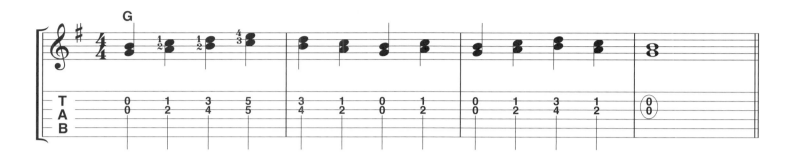

THE SLIDE

When notes are connected by a slanted line a technique called a slide is used. After the first note is played, the left-hand finger maintains pressure on the fretboard as it slides up or down to the next note. Do not pick the second note. Slides can be used to connect single notes and double stops.

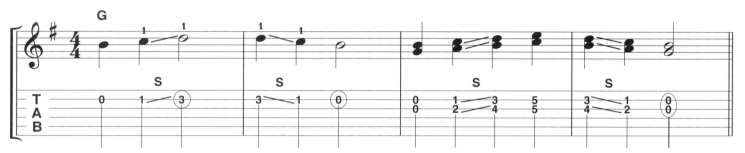

Can't Stop Me Now applies the slide technique to double stops.

21 Can't Stop Me Now

Oh you can't stop me now____ 'cause__ I'm leav-in' this town. And I

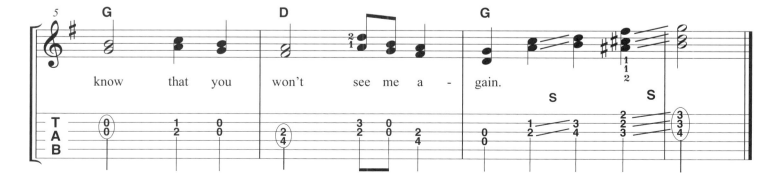

know that you won't see me a - gain.

Bury Me Beneath the Willow

Traditional

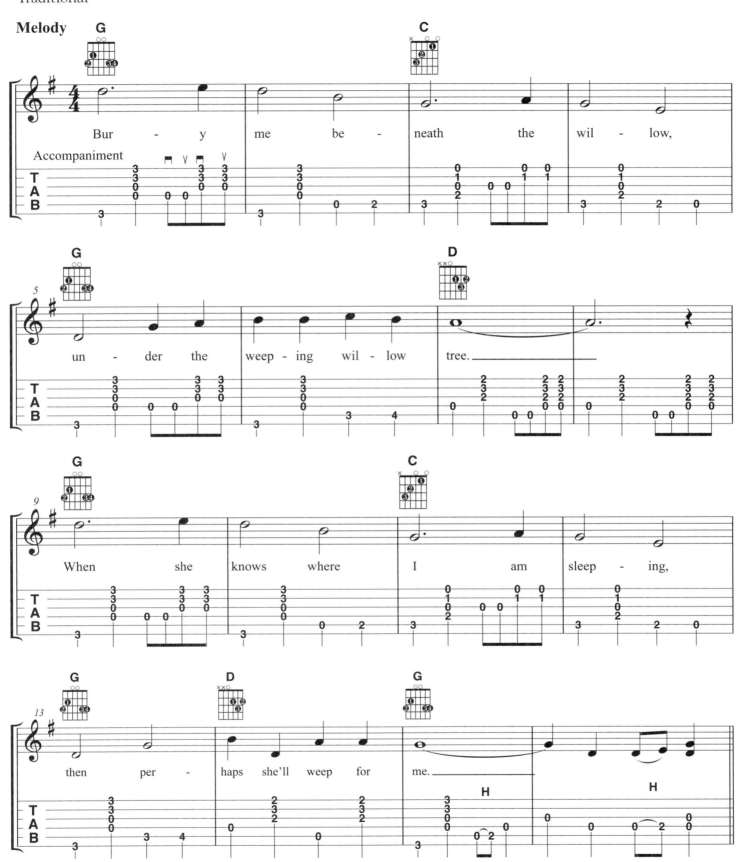

Melody

Bur - y me be - neath the wil - low,

Accompaniment

un - der the weep - ing wil - low tree.

When she knows where I am sleep - ing,

then per - haps she'll weep for me.

Take a little time to go over the new strum introduced in measure 1.
Use a down-up combination on the 5th of the chord followed by a
down-up on the top three strings.

G1053

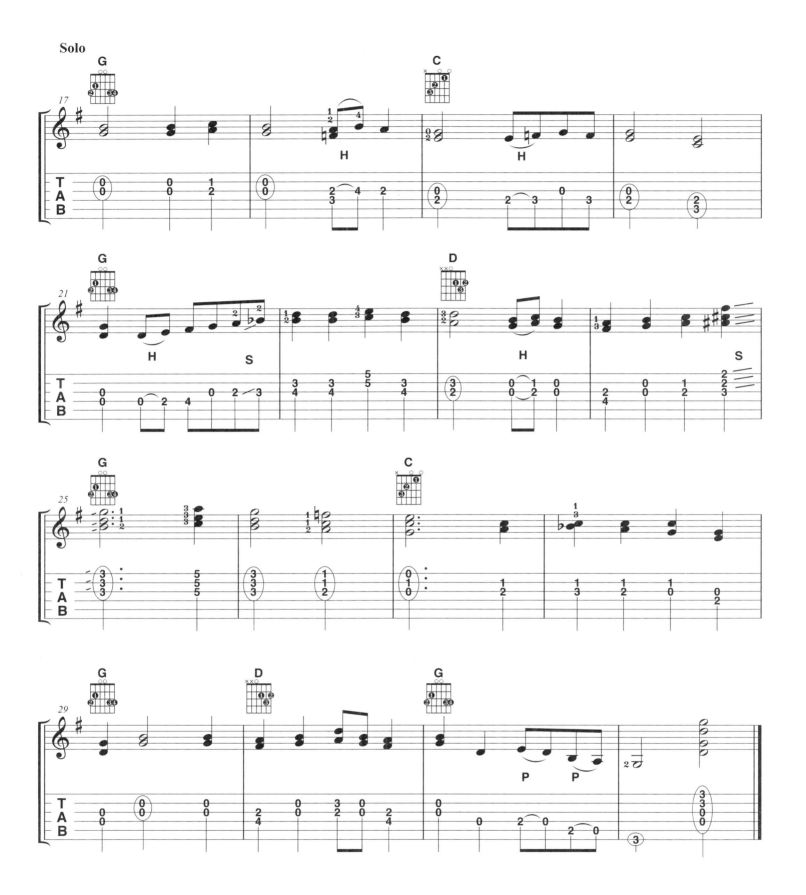

Bluegrass musicians usually end a song in one or two ways. *Bury Me Beneath the Willow* ends with a "let ring." Hold the final G chord for at least two beats or more.

Another option is the "cut off." To do a cut off, use both hands to abruptly **dampen** (stop from vibrating) all of the strings after using a forceful downstroke. This is usually a more effective ending in pieces that are in faster tempos.

The Capo

A capo allows you to play a song in a different key while using the same fingerings and chords you already know. This lets you stay in a position in which you are familiar. So if another player wants to play *Bury Me Beneath the Willow* (Key of G on pages 30-31) in the key of A, slap your capo on the second fret and you are ready to go. Just play as if you are in First Position.

Here is a chart that lets you know where to place your capo in the bluegrass friendly keys.

first position key	C	G	D	A	E
capo first fret	C♯/D♭	G♯/A♭	D♯/E♭	A/B♭	F
capo second fret	D	A	E	B	F♯/G♭
capo third fret	D♯/E♭	A♯/B♭	F	C	G
capo fourth fret	E	B	F♯/G♭	C♯/D♭	G♯/A♭
capo fifth fret	F	C	G	D	A

So, use your capo for three reasons:
1) You need to jam with another player but you do not know the song in a different key.
2) You want to sing but the vocal range is too low for your voice.
3) You want to experiment with different sounds.

Just for Fun

Have a good time with this fun-to-play progression
When you feel ready, play with the capo on the second fret. This version will be in the Key of _____ .

32

Guitar Solo

Capo 2, Key of _____?

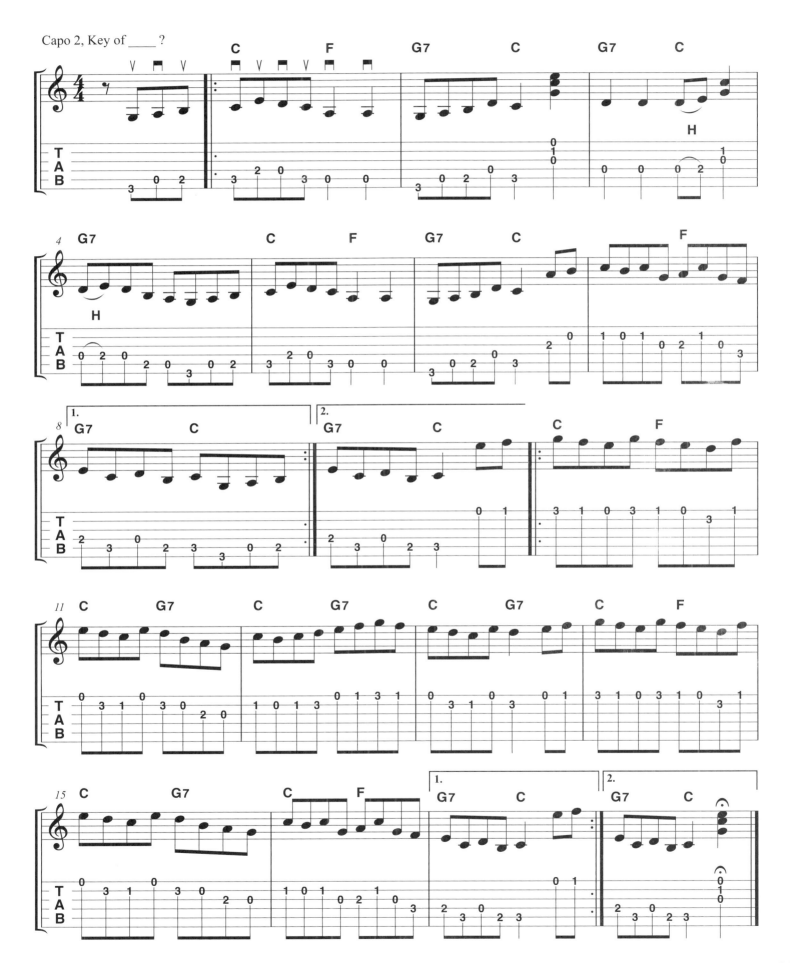

Blackberry Blossom

Traditional

Guitar Solo

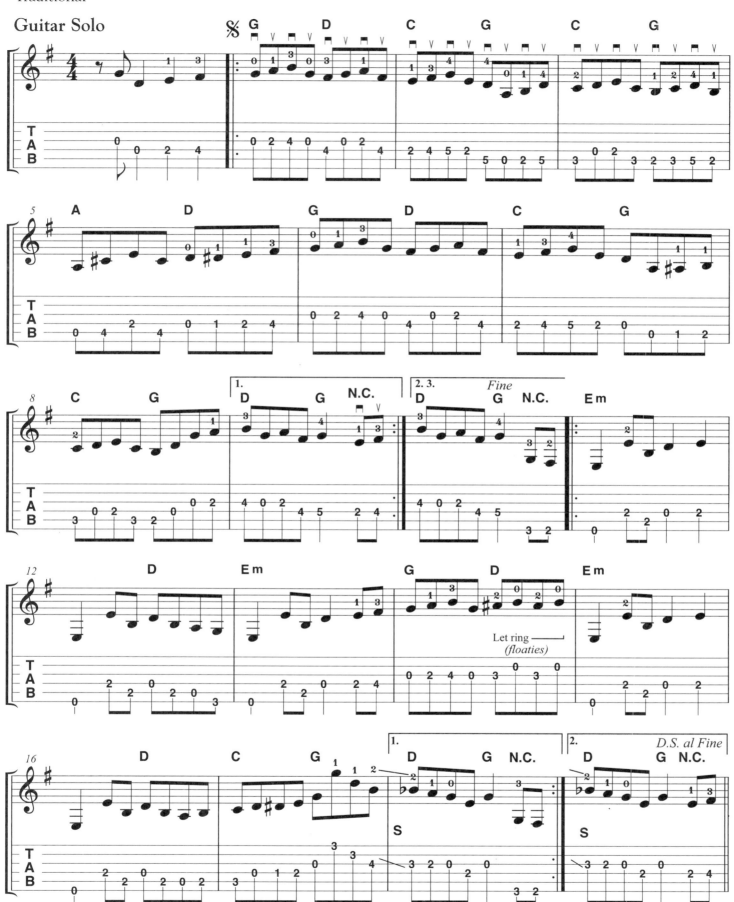

Kick It Off

Blackberry Blossom is another traditional fiddle tune that you *must* be familiar with.

G1053

Guitar Solo

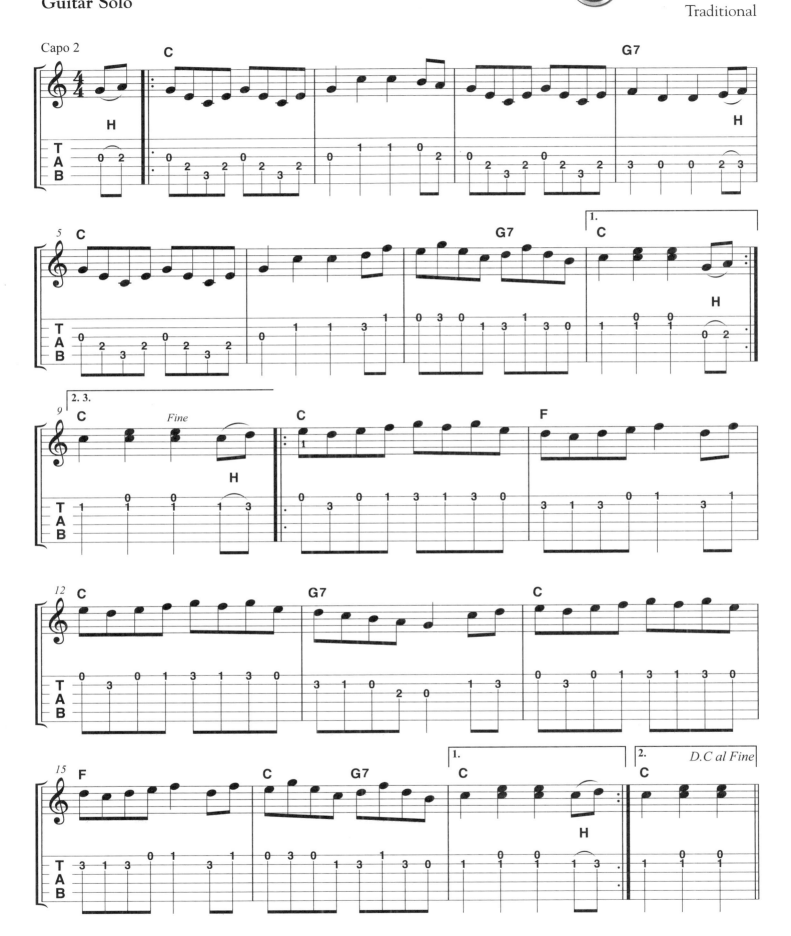

One Anna, Two Anna

Kick It Off

Many fiddle players kickoff a tune in a style similar to the first 4 measures of *One Anna, Two Anna*. When playing chords, come in at measure 5. This approach works well for guitar solos also.

PREPARING TO PLAY *SALLY GOODIN*

Playing two notes in a row that are the on the same fret, but adjacent strings, can seem tricky. The two examples below demonstrate different strategies for accomplishing this efficiently. Which version works best for you?

Choosing to move up the neck, instead of moving to the next string may increase speed and flow.

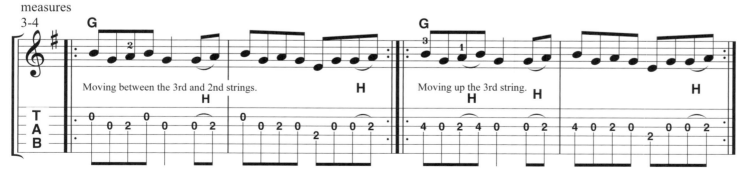

Left-hand fingering and fret choices play a big role in developing smooth, flowing solos, and in developing speed.

G1053

Guitar Solo

Sally Goodin

Traditional

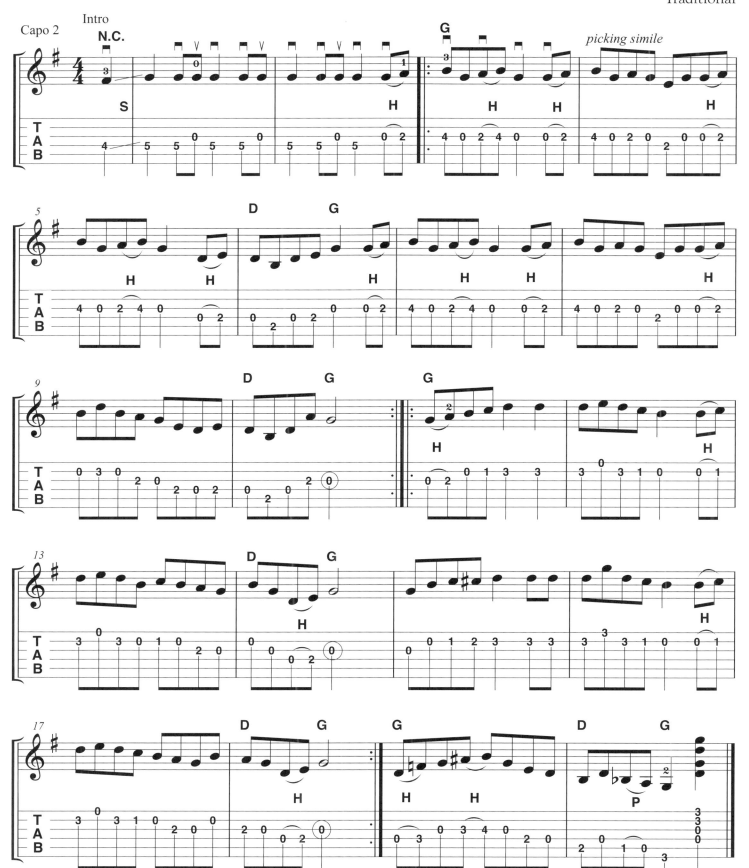

Crosspicking

Crosspicking is a popular technique among bluegrass guitarists. It involves playing individual strings of a chord as an accompaniment to melody notes, usually in a consistent pattern. There are many different approaches to crosspicking, and it is often interchanged with strummed chord accompaniment.

Play the following crosspicking exercise, paying close attention to pick direction. Form each chord and play from within the chord position as much as possible. The goal is to minimize left-hand movement.

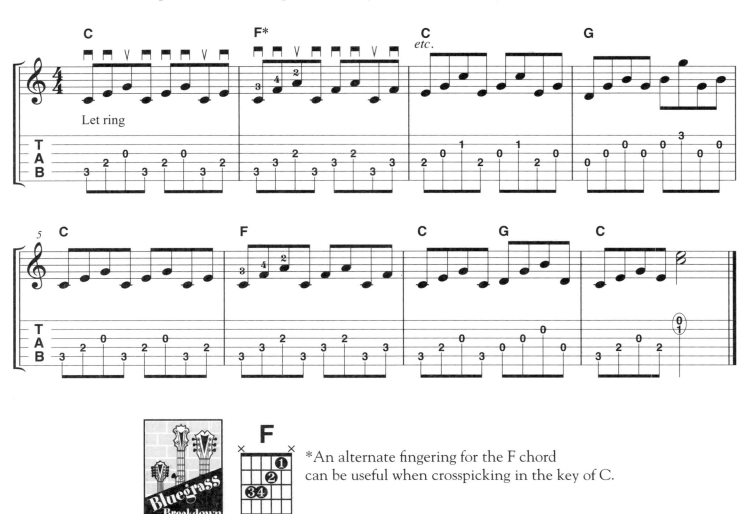

*An alternate fingering for the F chord can be useful when crosspicking in the key of C.

Crossing Little Creek ㉙

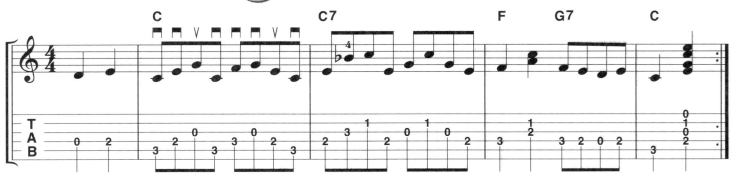

Kick It Off

one anna
two anna ...

Crossing Little Creek mixes melody, crosspicking, and strumming.

Kick It Off

Wildwood Flower is a tune made popular by the Carter Family.

Guitar Solo

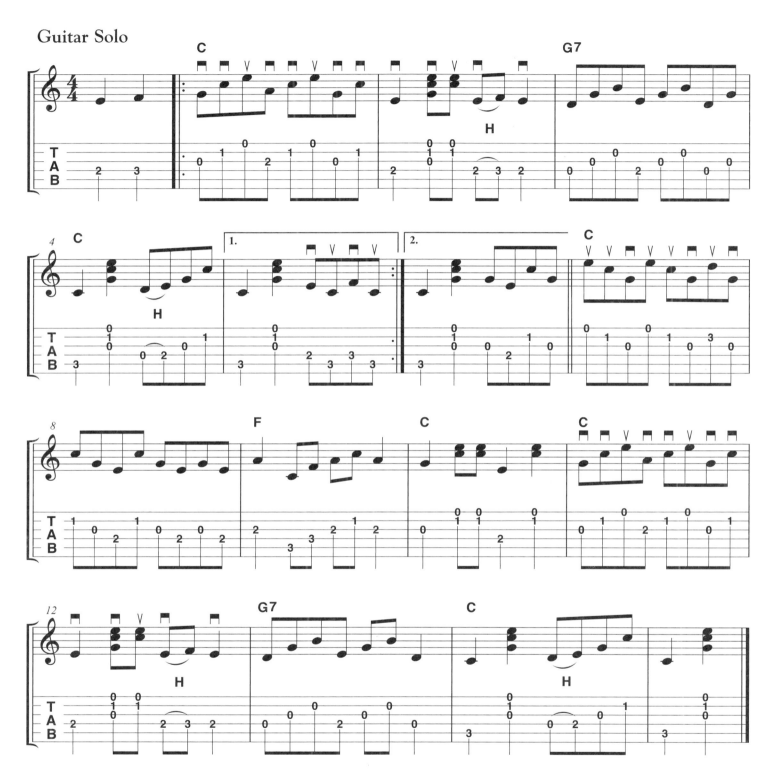

Create a new ending for *Wildwood Flower*.
Your choices are:

- C run
- Shave and a Haircut
- The JH lick on page 28
- A scale of your choice from page 21
- Your own ending

Shady Grove

Traditional

Intro

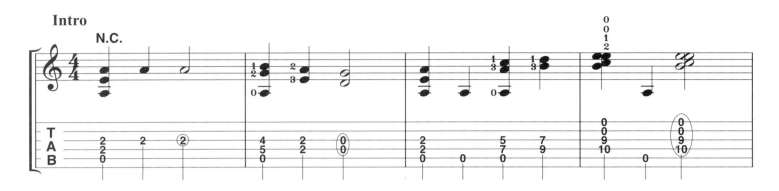

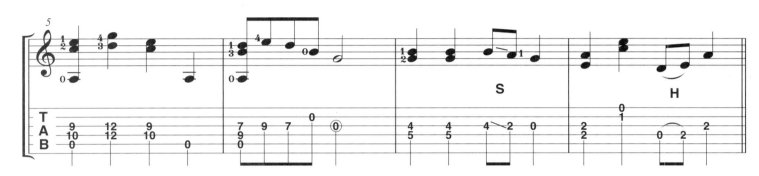

Verse and Chorus

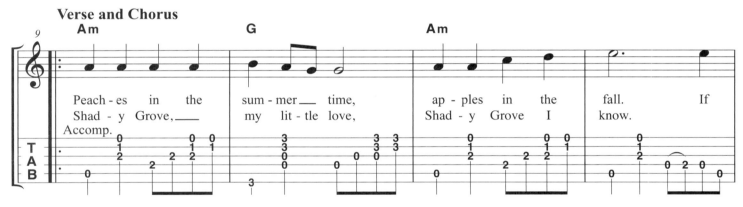

Peach - es in the sum - mer ___ time, ap - ples in the fall. If
Shad - y Grove, ___ my lit - tle love, Shad - y Grove I know.
Accomp.

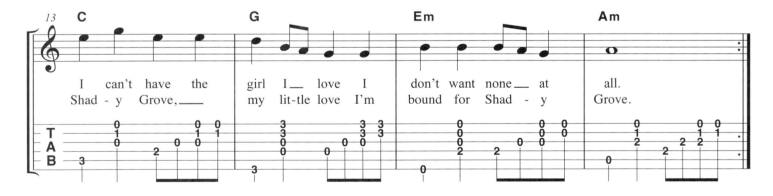

I can't have the girl I ___ love I don't want none ___ at all.
Shad - y Grove, ___ my lit - tle love I'm bound for Shad - y Grove.

There are many notes played in unusual places in this arrangement. Tony Rice uses this arranging technique in many of his solos.

G1053

Solo 1

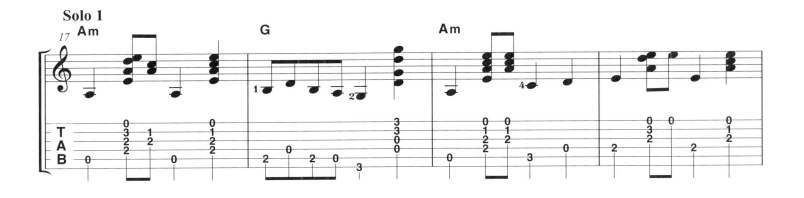

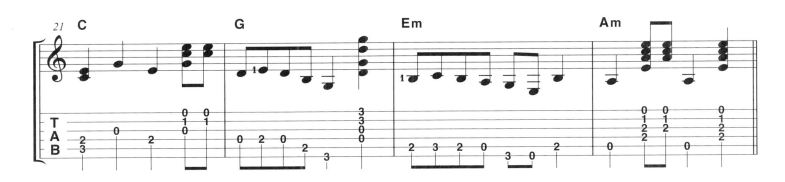

Solo 2

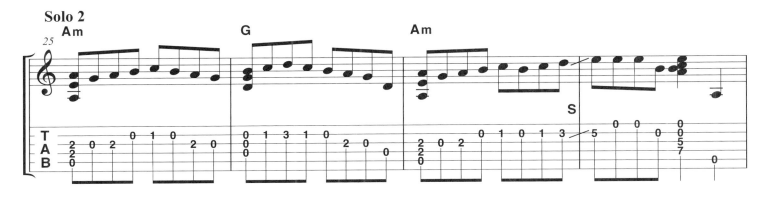

Kick It Off

one anna
two anna ...

Shady Grove is a favorite tune popular with folk, Celtic, and bluegrass musicians. Actually it is a song about a person, not a place.

Beaumont Crossing

Guitar Solo

Capo 2

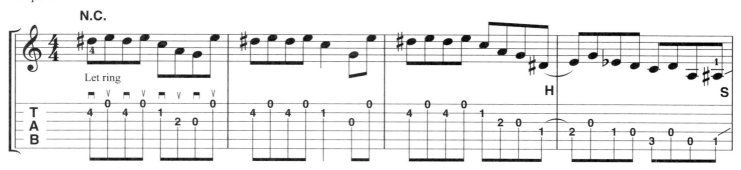

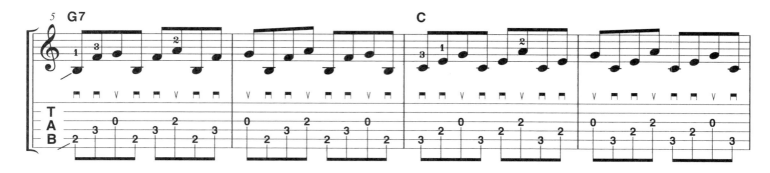

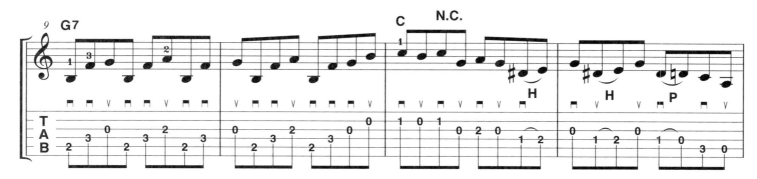

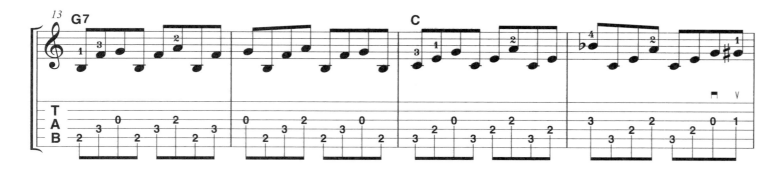

Kick It Off

one anna
two anna ...

Beaumont Crossing is based on the popular bluegrass tune *Beaumont Rag*. Bob Wills recorded a popular version and the contemporary rock group *Phish* has been known to play the tune in their live concerts.

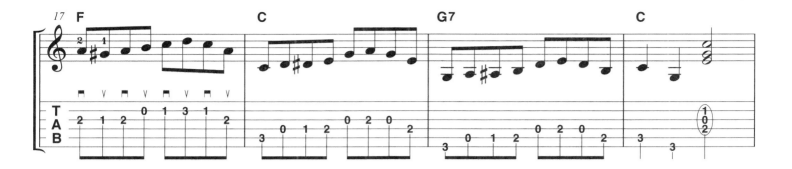

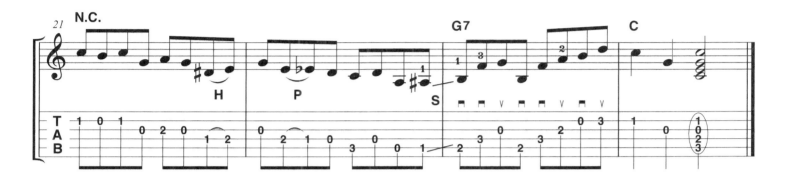

Many crosspicking examples can be found in *Beaumont Crossing*. Be sure to follow the picking patterns indicated in the music.

Song for the Doc

There is a lot of technique in this fun-to-play tune. Start slowly, be accurate, then speed it up! When you feel ready, play with the capo on the second fret. This version will be in the Key of _____ .

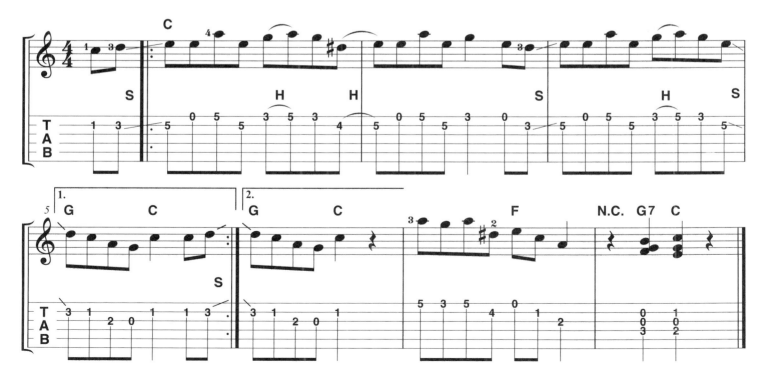

New River Train

Traditional

Kick It Off
one anna two anna ...

New River Train uses a chord-melody soloing style seen previously in *Under the Double Eagle* and *Shady Grove*. This style was made popular by the Carter Family, and is sometimes called "Carter Style" picking.

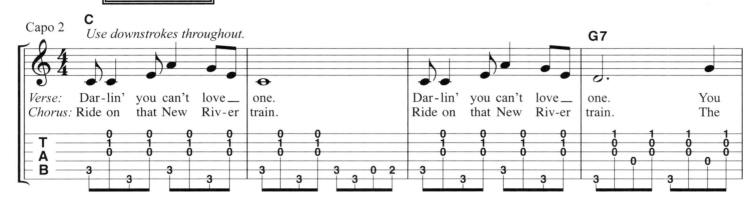

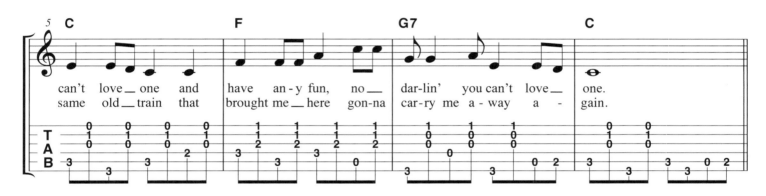

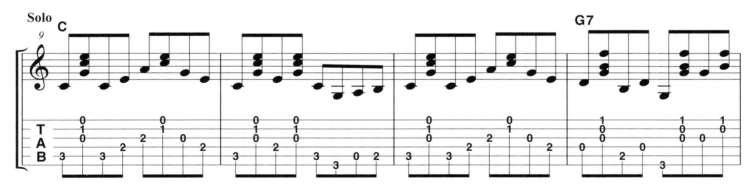

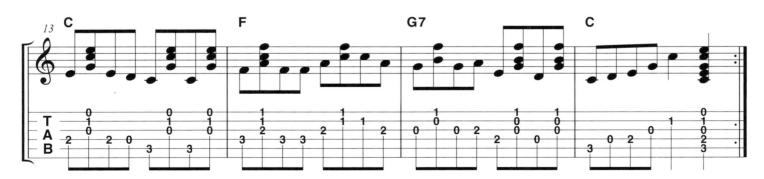

Trains are a popular subject in bluegrass music. Check out other popular train tunes like *Orange Blossom Special* and *Train 45*.

G1053

Beyond Tradition
Introducing The "9" Chord

The chords used in bluegrass accompaniment need not be limited to major, minor, and dominant seventh chords. Substituting chords with more musically colorful tones can add new and interesting sounds to traditional tunes. The 9 chord is used as a substitute for 7 chords by many modern bluegrass pickers.

Ninth chords are often used in jazz, and can give an element of jazziness to bluegrass tunes. Be careful, though, to use ninth chords only when you want that unique quality.

Take This Hammer

Traditional

Melody

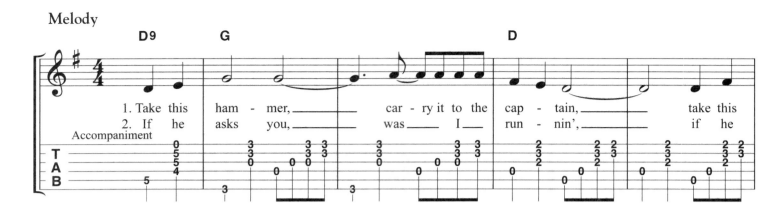

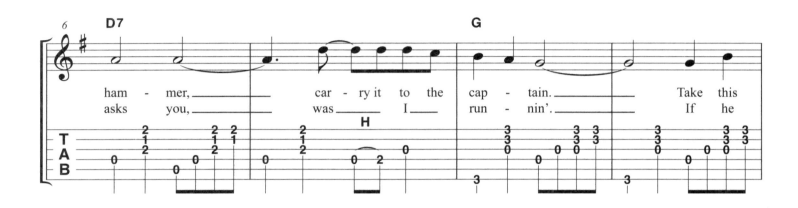

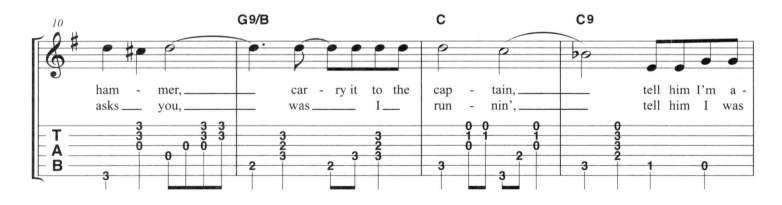

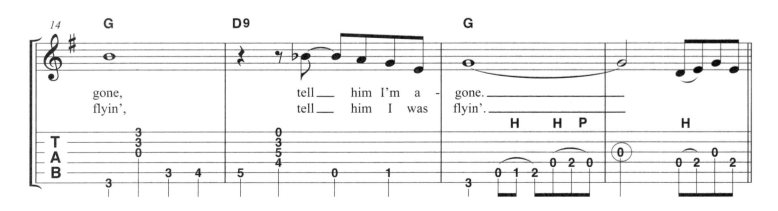

Solo

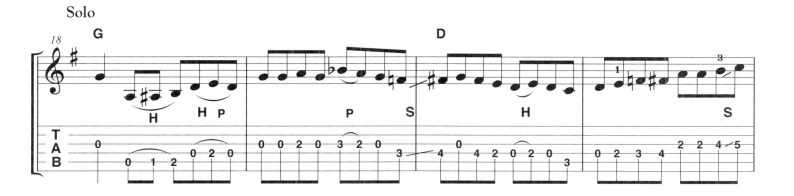

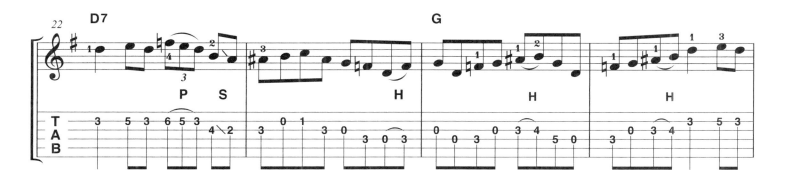

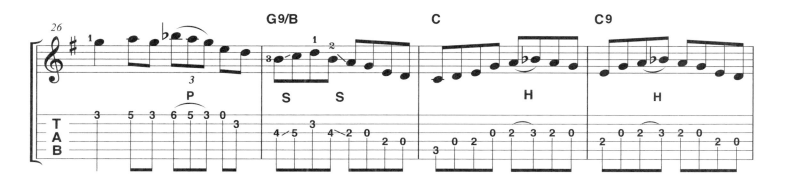

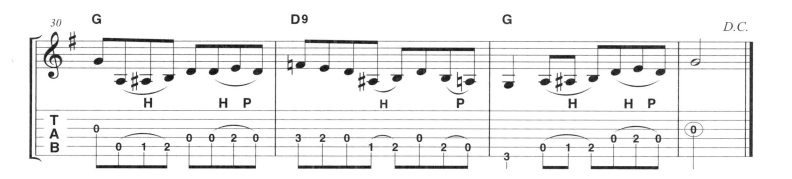

Hammer Songs
Hard labor involving the hammer in mining, railroads, and other major industries during the 19th century led to the creation of many traditional American songs known as "hammer songs."

One of the most famous, *Take This Hammer*, was recorded by popular bluegrass groups including Flatt and Scruggs, The Osborne Brothers, as well as blues legend, Leadbelly. Other hammer songs have become bluegrass standards as well. Perhaps the most famous is Merle Travis' version of *Nine Pound Hammer*.

Glossary

break refers to taking a solo in bluegrass music (page 20)

capo a device that allows you to easily raise the pitch of the open strings to play in a different key (page 3, 32)

crosspicking a favorite guitar style of bluegrass guitarists. This flatpicking style usually consists of three pitches repeating in a four-note rhythm. (page 38)

dampen lightly touching the strings to stop them from vibrating (page 26)

D.C. al Fine repeat by going back to the beginning and ending at the term Fine (FEE nay), the end (page 35)

D.S. al Fine repeat by going back to the sign (𝄋) and ending at the term Fine (FEE nay), the end (page 34)

doublestops playing two notes at a time (page 29)

dreadnought the body of a dreadnought guitar is larger than most guitars and has a bolder sound (page 3)

floaties a run that has open strings still ringing while playing fretted notes (page 26)

harmony musical notes sounded together; chords (page 29)

Key of C key signature (no sharps or flats), primary chords C F G (page 6)

Key of G key signature (one sharp, F♯), primary chords G C D (page 5)

melody a succession of notes that tells us "how the song goes," also referred to as the tune (page 7)

Let ring allow the strings to vibrate freely (page 26)

metronome a device that indicates how many beats there are in a minute (bpm) (page 26)

N.C. The term "No chord" indicates the rhythm instuments stop playing while the soloist continues. (page 20)

rhythm how the music moves in time; the beat (page 7)

run a series of notes that has an appealing sound; also called a lick or a riff (page 13)

G1053